WITHDRAWN

D0859063

IMAGES
of America

KMOX
THE VOICE OF ST. LOUIS

what makes
KMOX RADIO
total entertainment?❋

*BOB HARDY *JACK BUCK *HARRY CARAY *REX DAVIS
*DAN KELLY *JOHN McCORMICK *JIM BUTLER *HARRY FENDER
*JAMES WHITE *NELSON KIRKWOOD *BOB BURNES *RAY GERACY
*CHARLES HEFTI *Sgt. ED MOORE *J. ROY McCARTHY *BOB OSBORNE
*KEN BILLUPS *LAURENT TORNO
*DOUG NEWMAN *GUS KYLE

KMOX RADIO

This 1969 promotional brochure showcased many of the station's top personalities. (St. Louis Media Archive.)

ON THE COVER: The *Dorothy Perkins Program* broadcasts live from the KMOX Mart Building studios in the early 1930s. (Sue Dorn.)

IMAGES
of America

KMOX
THE VOICE OF ST. LOUIS

Frank Absher

ARCADIA
PUBLISHING

Copyright © 2012 by Frank Absher
ISBN 978-0-7385-9113-1

Published by Arcadia Publishing
Charleston, South Carolina

Printed in the United States of America

Library of Congress Control Number: 2011934090

For all general information, please contact Arcadia Publishing:
Telephone 843-853-2070
Fax 843-853-0044
E-mail sales@arcadiapublishing.com
For customer service and orders:
Toll-Free 1-888-313-2665

Visit us on the Internet at www.arcadiapublishing.com

To Jeff and Barbara, who kept telling me I "should write a book"

THE HOLDER OF THIS CARD IS CERTIFIED TO BE A
Regular Listening Member
1120 CLUB
and is at all times, during the existence of this organization, entitled to preferred rights in making requests for tunes to be played by KMOX on its program of this same name, provided all requests are made from the latest official selection list of the "Eleven-Twenty Club" and are accompanied by the number of this membership card.

Call CEntral 8245

No. **1355**
(Not Transferable)

Recording Secretary

Although KMOX was later known for a talk format that virtually excluded the playing of music, there was a time when the station actively took music requests. (St. Louis Media Archive.)

CONTENTS

ACKNOWLEDGMENTS

Happenstance got me involved in the radio business: the income from a disc jockey job helped me cover my college expenses. During those years, I set my sights on a career goal—I wanted to work at KMOX in St. Louis.

It had been the station my grandfather listened to religiously in a small Southern Illinois town, following his beloved St. Louis Cardinals. It was also the station my mother listened to on that radio perched atop the refrigerator.

Once I began working in the business, it was clear that KMOX was the one station that signified success in the industry. And I made it, 10 years after graduation.

Walking through those halls in the late 1970s was more than a dream come true. Those people whose voices had come out of the box on the refrigerator were now my coworkers, and at the ripe old age of 32, I was on the team.

The KMOX staff has always been populated by legends of the industry, and the station has won every major award in the radio business—some more than once.

KMOX: *The Voice of St. Louis* is a pictorial history of this legendary station. There were times when photographs were not taken or periods from which pictures cannot be located; however, the images that could be located and are of the quality needed for this book are assembled to provide a glimpse into the proud past of a radio station that was considered the crown jewel of CBS Radio.

Thanks to Jean Gosebrink, St. Louis Public Library Media Archive; Charles Brown, St. Louis Mercantile Library; Michael Henry, Library of American Broadcasting, University of Maryland; KMOX Radio; Molly Hyland; Sue Dorn; Therese Dickman, SIU-E Lovejoy Library: The St. Louis Media History Foundation; and Elizabeth Bray, authors' muse and editor at Arcadia Publishing.

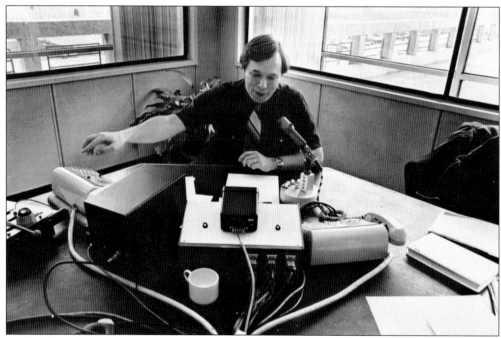

Author Frank Absher is shown hosting *At Your Service* in 1980. (St. Louis Media Archive.)

INTRODUCTION

A handful of St. Louisans were the only audience to hear the first radio broadcast originating in St. Louis on election night, November 2, 1920. Two young men, gifted in their knowledge of electronics, built an experimental transmitter in the basement of a home at 4312 DeTonty Street in South St. Louis and announced the vote totals, which were provided by the St. Louis *Post-Dispatch*.

Within two years, that newspaper had built its own radio station and received a license from the federal government to operate it. St. Louis University also put a station on the air, and KSD and WEW became the first licensed radio stations in St. Louis.

In the early 1920s, the radio industry was chaotic, to say the least. Because there was no technical oversight, many stations occupied the same frequency (dial position), which brought about a lot of jousting among them to determine which station would go on at what time.

By late 1925, seven more stations had signed on in St. Louis: KFUO, owned by the Lutheran Church—Missouri Synod; WEB, owned by the Benson brothers; KFVE, owned by the Film Corporation of America; WMAY, owned by the Kingshighway Presbyterian Church; KFWF, owned by the St. Louis Truth Center; KFQA, owned by The Principia; and WCK, owned by the Stix, Baer, and Fuller department store. In that year, two of those stations changed their call letters—WEB became WIL, and WCK became WSBF—but major changes for St. Louis radio were on the horizon.

A group of local business leaders came up with the idea of creating a radio superstation that would be powerful enough to be heard all over the United States. These businessmen reasoned such a broadcast giant would put the city of St. Louis on the map, equating the city with New York and Chicago. A quality radio station with a powerful signal would spread the word that St. Louis was a commercial force.

These men were willing to put up the money to make things happen. Their companies became shareholders in the new station: the St. Louis Merchants Exchange, *Globe-Democrat*, Brown Shoe Company, Kennedy Corporation, Skouras Brothers, C.F. Blanke Company, Kilgen and Son, Wagner Electric, the Radio Trades Association, Davis Realty and Mortgage Company, Mayfair Investment Company, Mississippi Valley Trust, Stark Brothers Nurseries and Orchards, F.C. Taylor Fur Company, and St. Louis Southwestern Railway. They named their organization the Voice of St. Louis, Inc.

A forward-thinking realty company donated some rural acreage in suburban Kirkwood as a site for the station's transmitter building and towers. The Mayfair Investment Company came up with studio space on the mezzanine of its new Mayfair Hotel in downtown St. Louis. The *Globe-Democrat* provided ample publicity as the station progressed through the planning and construction phases toward its projected sign-on date.

As summer temperatures slowly descended into autumn in St. Louis, the public became more and more curious about this big, new radio station. Kirkwood's Ridgeview subdivision, which consisted of vacant fields near the intersection of Geyer and Manchester roads at that time, became the destination of weekend adventurers on their autumnal Sunday joy rides as the people watched the station's two towers go up and the state-of-the-art transmitter building take shape. The October ground-breaking ceremony in that Kirkwood field attracted over 1,000 spectators.

More than a dozen people spoke that day. They represented the Voice of St. Louis, Inc. and the city of Kirkwood, and all extolled the value of a radio station that would reach the far corners of the United States. The *Globe-Democrat* gave the event front-page coverage the next day.

Station investors would end up getting more than just good publicity, however. Each company was to be provided with airtime on the station to do whatever it wanted, and the programs usually involved promoting the companies in some way. Later, as the station moved through its early years, investors sold their shares, which brought about an evolution of the St. Louis superstation to the status the owners had originally sought—a true national powerhouse.

With the sign-on date approaching, the organization applied for permission to use the call letters KVSL in honor of the Voice of St. Louis, but the government rejected that request. The second request was for KMO, but that sequence was already assigned. The third request was accepted, and KMOX was officially assigned to St. Louis. The call letter sequence had no special meaning, as did some others around the country. In Chicago, for example, WLS, owned by Sears, Roebuck, was said to stand for the "World's Largest Store," and WGN, owned by the *Chicago Tribune*, stood for "World's Greatest Newspaper."

The owners established a target date of December 24, 1925, for the station's sign-on, with regular programming to begin January 4, 1926, and, as might be expected, there was plenty of pomp and ceremony during the Christmas Eve broadcast. Of the many speeches by dignitaries, there was one that stood out for the fact that it gave birth to an urban legend of sorts.

E. Lansing Ray, who was the president and editor of the St. Louis *Globe-Democrat* and chairman of the board of directors of the Voice of St. Louis, Inc., reportedly used his remarks that night to proclaim that KMOX was St. Louis's Christmas gift to the United States. Later, some people swore that this explained the call letter sequence: "K" for Kirkwood; "MO" for Missouri; and "X" for Xmas Eve. While it sounds interesting, it simply wasn't true. The next morning's edition of the *Globe-Democrat* posted the front-page headline, " 'Voice of St. Louis' Formally Takes Air as Gift to America," an expansion of Ray's remarks.

The station's inaugural broadcast, which stretched past midnight and into Christmas morning, culminated with the dance music of the Gene Rodemich Jazz Orchestra, followed by two programs produced by two other St. Louis radio stations, WSBF and WIL.

Following the Christmas Eve broadcast, the radio station went through 11 days of practice broadcasts, which was common then, especially when the station broadcast with 5,000 watts of power, which was uncommonly high. That wattage achieved huge coverage for the station, as described in an article from the *Globe-Democrat*: "Telegrams and letters from every state in the Union and from many places outside the United States, including Canada, Mexico, Alaska and the Hawaiian Islands testify as to the ability of this station to penetrate into the far distant areas with great power and clarity."

It was under these conditions and into this environment that KMOX became a reality. Its future would see economic doldrums, wars, and the development of newer ways to communicate to the masses, but through its existence, KMOX has remained the Voice of St. Louis.

Thomas Patrick Convey is credited with organizing and managing the Voice of St. Louis, Inc. and was hired as the station's first manager. (St. Louis Media Archive.)

One

EARLY RADIO DAYS

The Mayfair Hotel at Ninth
and St. Charles Streets in
downtown St. Louis was the
first home to KMOX. Studios
were on the building's mezzanine
level. (The Roberts Mayfair,
A Wyndham Hotel.)

hotel **Mayfair** AT EIGHTH AND ST. CHARLES

DOWNTOWN ST. LOUIS AT YOUR DOORSTEP

Postcards like the one seen here were mailed out to promote the station. (St. Louis Media Archive.)

The KMOX transmission tower complex was in a field north of suburban Kirkwood. Transmission equipment was housed in the building. (St. Louis Media Archive.)

A large artists' reception room at the Mayfair studios was set aside for auditions and also was a gathering place for station visitors. Studios were seen through the double-glass windows. (St. Louis Mercantile Library Association.)

The first KMOX transmitter was a huge, state-of-the-art 5,000-watt Western Electric 104-A. It required on-site operation by several engineers. (St. Louis Media Archive.)

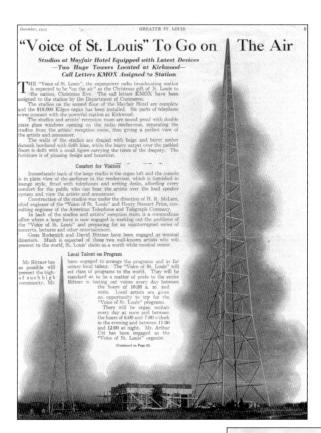

"Voice of St. Louis" To Go on The Air

Studios at Mayfair Hotel Equipped with Latest Devices —Two Huge Towers Located at Kirkwood— Call Letters KMOX Assigned to Station

THE "Voice of St. Louis", the superpower radio broadcasting station is expected to be "on the air" as the Christmas gift of St. Louis to the nation, Christmas Eve. The call letters KMOX have been assigned to the station by the Department of Commerce.

The studios on the second floor of the Mayfair Hotel are complete and the $18,000 Kilgen organ has been installed. Six parts of telephone wires connect with the powerful station at Kirkwood.

The studios and artists' reception room are sound proof with double plate glass windows opening on the radio rendezvous, separating the studios from the artists' reception room, thus giving a perfect view of the artists and announcer.

The walls of the studios are draped with beige and burnt umber damask bordered with delft blue, while the heavy carpet over the padded floors is delft with a small figure carrying the tones of the drapery. The furniture is of pleasing design and luxurious.

Comfort for Visitors

Immediately back of the large studio is the organ loft and the console is in plain view of the audience in the rendezvous, which is furnished in lounge style, fitted with telephones and writing desks, affording every comfort for the public who can hear the artists over the loud speaker system and, view the artists and announcer.

Construction of the studios was under the direction of H. R. McLain, chief engineer of the "Voice of St. Louis" and Henry Stewart Prior, consulting engineer of the American Telephone and Telegraph Company.

In back of the studios and artists' reception room is a commodious office where a large force is now engaged in working out the problems of the "Voice of St. Louis" and preparing for an uninterrupted series of concerts, lectures and other entertainment.

Gene Rodemich and David Bittner have been engaged as musical directors. Much is expected of these two well-known artists who will present to the world, St. Louis' claim as a worth while musical center

Local Talent on Program

Mr. Bittner has as possible will present the high-of such high community. Mr. been engaged to arrange the programs and as far secure local talent. The "Voice of St. Louis" will est class of programs to the world. They will be standard as to be a matter of pride to the entire Bittner is testing out voices every day between the hours of 10:30 a. m. and noon. Local artists are given an opportunity to try for the "Voice of St. Louis" programs.

There will be organ recitals every day at noon and between the hours of 6:00 and 7:00 o'clock in the evening and between 11:30 and 12:00 at night. Mr. Arthur Utt has been engaged as the "Voice of St. Louis" organist.

(Continued on Page 20)

Prior to signing on, the station's owners generated mounds of publicity all over the United States, such as this article in *Greater St. Louis Magazine*. (St. Louis Media Archive.)

Engineers at the transmitter site used this master control position to communicate with the studio downtown and make necessary technical adjustments to maximize the station's signal quality. (St. Louis Media Archive.)

Beige and burnt umber curtain material covered the Mayfair studios' walls and ceilings for soundproofing, and there was heavy carpeting on the floors to prevent any sound reflection. (KMOX.)

The Kirkwood transmitter site, known to the locals as Jelly Roll Hill, was literally a rural setting. The large land area was needed so copper wire could be buried as an electrical grounding system. (St. Louis Media Archive.)

The KMOX house orchestra was conducted by David Bittner, one of the station's music directors. (KMOX Music Collection, LIS, Lovejoy Library, SIU-Edwardsville.)

Herbert Berger was the leader of the orchestra at the Coronado Hotel. The group was sometimes called the St. Louis Club Orchestra. KMOX listeners frequently heard the band on remote broadcasts in the 1920s. (St. Louis Media Archive.)

The *Globe-Democrat*, one of the Voice of St. Louis, Inc. investors, used its Sunday edition in 1927 to promote the station by treating fans to caricatures of favorite station personalities. (St. Louis Media Archive.)

ST. LOUIS, SUNDAY MORNING, JANUARY 30, 1927.

KMOX'S Staff in Sketch and Caricature

ALICE MASLIN
Program Director

BILL WEST
Supervising Engineer

JACQUINOT JULES
Musical Director

COLLEGIATE

GEORGE JUNKIN
Director- Announcer -

MEL DIX
Assistant Announcer

"TORCHY"
Our Red Headed Syncopation

"BOB"
ROBERT M. REED -
Publicity Director

ANN WALSH
Studio Director

Ken Barker

Red and Green were musical artists on KMOX during the station's early days, sponsored by Stark Brothers' Nurseries, one of the Voice of St. Louis shareholders. (St. Louis Media Archive.)

AMERICAN COMMERCIAL PHOTOGRAPHERS, ST. LOUIS, MO.

Bill Mack set out to make a name for himself reporting sports on KMOX. He paid his own way to spring training in Florida in the late 1920s to provide coverage on KMOX by telegraphing his reports back to the station. Mack is also credited with founding the KMOX *Hot Stove League* program, but when he was passed over for the station's baseball play-by-play job, he left to work at another radio station. (St. Louis Media Archive.)

OUR RECORD-BREAKING
ST. LOUIS ROBIN
AND ITS INTREPID PILOTS
Every Detail Broadcast
OVER
KMOX

FOREST O'BRINE

ALE JACKSON

KMOX gave extensive coverage to the St. Louis team involved in an aerial endurance competition in July 1929. Two teams in other cities eventually dropped out, and local pilots Dale Jackson and Forest O'Brine took the $31,000 prize for staying aloft for 420 hours and 21 minutes. A crowd estimated at 15,000 journeyed to Lambert field to greet the two after KMOX announced a planned landing time. (St. Louis Media Archive.)

His given name was Chester Gruber, but on KMOX, he was known as "Tony Cabooch." Gruber's background was in vaudeville, and he came to KMOX with a stable of characters he had created with different dialects. In his first 14 weeks on the station, he received 42,000 fan letters. By 1930, Anheuser-Busch had agreed to sponsor his show on the CBS Radio Network, paying him $500 a week for a 26-week run of the *Anheuser-Busch Antics*. (St. Louis Media Archive.)

Program host Harry "Pappy" Cheshire poses with two of his show's personalities—comedian/musician Ambrose Haley and Baby Mary Lou. (St. Louis Media Archive.)

This KMOX microphone, one of the station's first mikes, was used in countless publicity photographs in the 1920s and 1930s. (St. Louis Media Archive.)

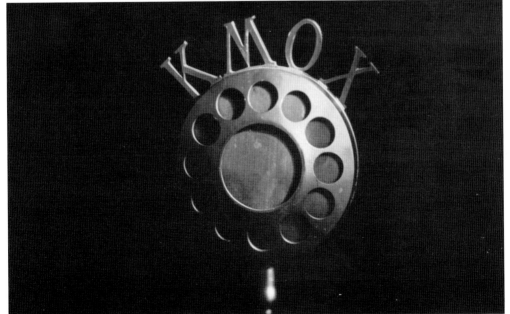

In 1928, KMOX began a series of technical changes. As the station began the next decade during a period of severe national economic instability, CBS purchased complete ownership of KMOX and increased the station's broadcast power to 50,000 watts. A new transmitter site was chosen, and the Kirkwood site was sold to another St. Louis radio station, KWK. (St. Louis Media Archive.)

In 1930, the station moved its transmitter site to far south St. Louis County in the Meramec Valley on Baumgartner Road. At the same time, a new, more powerful transmitter and tower system were installed, making KMOX the first CBS-owned station to broadcast with 50,000 watts of power. A special water-cooled system had been installed during the building's construction to help keep the massive electronic equipment from overheating. (St. Louis Mercantile Library Association.)

The Voice of St. Louis Inc.

Studios and Offices

HOTEL MAYFAIR

SAINT LOUIS
U.S.A.

With the continued growth of the radio industry, it had become clear that KMOX had outgrown its original studio facilities. (St. Louis Media Archive.)

After five years occupying the mezzanine level of the downtown Mayfair Hotel, KMOX moved a few blocks south. (The Roberts Mayfair, A Wyndham Hotel.)

Two

KMOX DURING THE GREAT DEPRESSION

MARTS BUILDING, ST. LOUIS, MO.—99

Amid a great deal of justifiable hoopla, KMOX moved into its new headquarters in the newly constructed 20-story Mart Building in December 1931. CBS now had all the parts in place for its new superstation. (St. Louis Media Archive.)

Located at Twelfth and Spruce streets in downtown St. Louis, the newly constructed Mart Building became the second home of KMOX. (St. Louis Media Archive.)

This grand staircase greeted visitors as they entered the Mart Building off Twelfth Street. The doors at the top led into the station's ornate reception room. CBS invested over $250,000 in construction of the new facility, with all construction work being done during the heart of the Great Depression. The station's studios and offices occupied 25,000 square feet on two floors of the building. Above the double doors at the top of the stairs, metal letters on the wood-panel wall spelled out "CBS—KMOX—The Voice of St. Louis—The Columbia Broadcasting System." Shown posing on the stairs for a publicity photograph is the Pappy Cheshire hillbilly group. (St. Louis Media Archive.)

The reception area at the top of the winding staircase was decorated with murals that depicted the history of St. Louis, including an airplane flying over the ocean, a tribute to Charles Lindbergh. CBS built the studios to provide the network with a new, major program production facility, from which hundreds of programs were beamed to the network. Another set of double doors behind the receptionist's desk opened into a long hallway. (St. Louis Media Archive.)

A total of five radio broadcast and rehearsal studios and a newsroom lined both sides of the hallway, in addition to the large auditorium studio at the hallway's end. The station's many visitors could watch much of the activity through the double-glass windows. (St. Louis Media Archive.)

In the station's main auditorium and studio, which could seat an audience of 700, a main stage was built to approximate a theater setting. (St. Louis Mercantile Library Association.)

One of the station's signature groups throughout the 1930s was the Ozark Mountaineers hillbilly band. Shown in this photograph with station farm director Charley Stookey (seated, center), the group was a mainstay over many years of programming directed toward the large farm audience. (St. Louis Media Archive.)

By far, the single most talked-about group on KMOX was Pappy Cheshire's group. They were heard early in the morning and late at night, with virtually every program broadcast live. Cheshire, shown dressed in white, was a showman with Hollywood aspirations who gave many of his performers their first big break. His program was sponsored for many years by Uncle Dick Slack's Furniture Store. (St. Louis Media Archive.)

One of those whose careers got a boost on KMOX was comedian George Gobel, shown here as teenage hillbilly comic George Goebel. (St. Louis Media Archive.)

Goebel's stay at KMOX was relatively short. He was also on the WLS Barndance. In an interview later in his career, he referenced his work in St. Louis, saying "We really had some times. Boy!" (St. Louis Media Archive.)

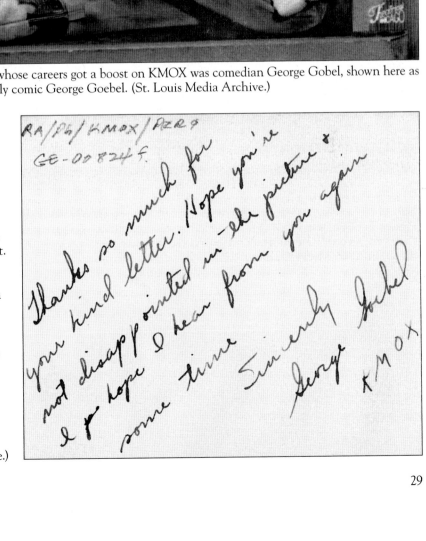

RAY PERIANDRI   ROY QUEEN   WESLEY HOWE

"SKEETS" YANEY   WADE RAY   TOMMY WATSON   "SMILIE" SUTTER

LES MAYBERRY   LAMBERT KAIMAN   MOSE   "RUSTY" MARION

ALISANDRO   JUDY   SALLY   JUNE   "SHUCKS" AUSTIN

Many of the people shown in this photograph of the Wade Ray band were also members of Pappy Cheshire's group, including Ray himself. Because of this sort of musical cross-pollination, the groups could present programs on a six-day-a-week basis and not have to worry if a couple members were not available. (St. Louis Media Archive.)

KMOX was the first radio job for Wade Ray. At age 18, he immediately became a member of the Pappy Cheshire Group. By that time, he was already an experienced performer, having played at county fairs in his home state of Arkansas and in Vaudeville. (St. Louis Media Archive.)

A separate studio was constructed as part of the Mart Building complex to house the huge organ, which was used for musical programs and providing musical bridges. (St. Louis Media Archive.)

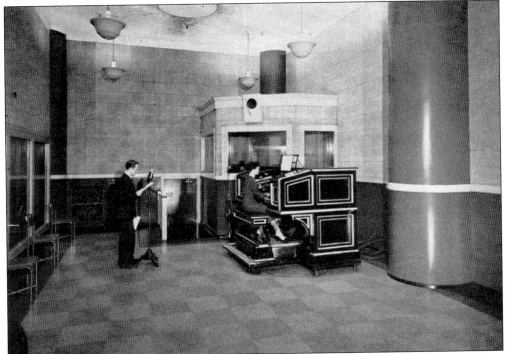

Pappy Cheshire was nothing if not a promoter. He called his group the National Champion Hillbillies, and even though personnel changed, the group remained the most popular musical organization on KMOX for many years. A former member told of the nights when the band would play a country fair in Central Missouri or Southern Illinois and jump into their cars to race back to the KMOX studios in time for their early morning radio performance. (St. Louis Media Archive.)

Charley Stookey came to KMOX in 1932 as the station's farm director and spent a total of six years with the station. He was responsible for the early morning programming, which involved farm reports, live hillbilly music, and comedy. Stookey also reported on regional agriculture developments for CBS Network farm programs. (St. Louis Media Archive.)

Not all hillbilly singers performed in a group. Melody Ann was a solo act. (St. Louis Media Archive.)

Members of the Sons of the Prairie Monte Rhine, Curley Roberts, Frankie Townsend, and Smokey Smith were each also part of other KMOX groups. (St. Louis Media Archive.)

Roy Queen began as a group member but also branched out and performed as a soloist. (St. Louis Media Archive.)

Lullaby Lester Mayberry later followed in the footsteps of his cousin Roy Queen and became a KMOX performer. (St. Louis Media Archive.)

KMOX COUNTRY JOURNAL ENTERTAINERS
Reading from left to right, standing: Lester "Lullaby" Mayberrie, Eddie "Catfish" Gentry, Stuffy Austin, Brother Bob Hastings.
Sitting: Wade Ray.

The *KMOX Country Journal*, hosted by Charley Stookey, featured all these men from other groups in yet another iteration as a hillbilly group led by fiddler Wade Ray. Standing are Lester Mayberry, Eddie Gentry, Stuffy Austin, and Robert Hastings. Wade Ray is seated. (St. Louis Media Archive.)

Aaron Jordan went by the stage name "Dixie Boy." (St. Louis Media Archive.)

Even as a soloist, Eddie Gentry was known by his stage name, "Catfish." (St. Louis Media Archive.)

Like many of the KMOX hillbilly performers, Roy Fields began working at the station as a teenager and was a member of several groups. (St. Louis Media Archive.)

Duo Viola and Eddie featured a woman playing steel slide guitar. (St. Louis Media Archive.)

Ambrose Haley provided the bass line and comedy for several KMOX hillbilly groups. (St. Louis Media Archive.)

Jimmie Pierson and Dick Klasi performed as a comedy musical duet, the Novelty Boys. (St. Louis Media Archive.)

Baby Mary Lou was part of the National Champion Hillbillies group for several years. (St. Louis Media Archive.)

The Kasper Sisters performed as a duet and with other groups on various programs. (St. Louis Media Archive.)

Helen Graham was the Ozark Sweetheart, starting her career on KMOX at age 14. Helen's younger sister Pat recalls a backyard filled with musicians at their South St. Louis home, rehearsing for the radio shows. When the weather was too cold, they rehearsed inside while the girls' mother ironed clothes and little sister Pat sang along. (St. Louis Media Archive.)

As she got older, Helen was a frequent soloist. Much later, she provided the yodeling voice heard on the first commercials for Busch Bavarian Beer. It was at KMOX that she met accordion player Roy Fields, her future husband. Helen and Roy left KMOX when an Indiana station made a better financial offer. (St. Louis Media Archive.)

Cousin Emmy (Cynthia Mae Carver) developed a strong following as a performer on KMOX. A website by Mark Hayes reports she was dubbed the "most-perfect singer of mountain ballads" by the St. Louis City Art Museum. *Time* magazine wrote that she played 15 different instruments on her program, which was heard on KMOX at 5:25 each Sunday morning. (St. Louis Media Archive.)

In Fun
Patsy

California Studio

Patsy Woodward was the comedic character known as Patsy the Pest for several years on the *Uncle Dick Slack* radio program featuring Pappy Cheshire's National Champion Hillbillies. She can also be seen in costume in the group photographs on pages 24, 28, and 32. (St. Louis Media Archive.)

Activity on the large stage in the KMOX Mart Building theater provided many entertaining moments for the audience. Backstage antics also proved entertaining, as this photograph shows. During rehearsal time, some serious horsing around resulted in Roy Queen losing his shirt. (St. Louis Media Archive.)

Sometime after the backstage antics, the group got together to rehearse prior to airtime. Seated at far left is Skeets Yaney. The Miccolis Sisters are also seen seated and studying their material. The staff announcer at far left, Bob Holt, uses a music stand to hold his script and program lineup. Note that the performers are all in their full performance dress, even though it was a radio show. (St. Louis Media Archive.)

Frankie and Skeets pose with Pappy Cheshire. *Billboard* magazine wrote in 1944, "Clyde 'Skeets' Yaney and Frankie Taylor are the very popular radio team of Skeets and Frankie, stars of Pappy Cheshire's Gang of Radio Station KMOX in St. Louis. They have been together 14 years . . . Both sing and play the guitar, harmonizing splendidly . . . Stars of Station KMOX and the Columbia Net." (St. Louis Media Archive.)

Frankie (left) and Skeets were such strong performers, they enjoyed a successful career as a duet after Pappy left the station. (St. Louis Media Archive.)

Three

MORE THAN HILLBILLIES

The large number of hillbilly groups and programs on KMOX provided the station ample opportunity for external promotion, such as the songbook shown here. But KMOX was also known for much more than hillbilly music. The studios were built by CBS to serve as an origination point for live programming of all kinds to be broadcast to the nation.

A special nationwide broadcast produced on KMOX began at midnight the evening of December 6, 1933, in commemoration of the end of Prohibition. Announcer France Laux (left) stood by at the Anheuser-Busch Brewery as topper August A. "Gussie" Busch Jr. used the network airwaves to urge Americans to once again enjoy a good, wholesome glass of beer. (Anheuser-Busch.)

KMOX
THE VOICE OF ST. LOUIS

50,000 WATT KEY STATION
COLUMBIA BROADCASTING SYSTEM

*90 Kilo
*2.1 Meters

December 21, 1933
Vol. 1—Number 2

BUDWEISER ON THE AIR!!

ANHEUSER-BUSCH SPONSORS
ST. LOUIS SYMPHONY ON KMOX

Sponsored by Anheuser-Busch, the St. Louis Symphony Orchestra with Vladimir Golschmann conducting, will present a full hour program over KMOX Sunday, Dec. 24, at 5:45 P.M.

Program is a trial. There will be no commercial blurbs. Mr. August A. Busch, Jr., will introduce the program in a brief talk, and Mr. Arthur Gaines, manager of the St. Louis Symphony Society, will act as announcer.

— KMOX —

NEW BOOM AND BANG MAN AT KMOX

Phil Silverson, who started in radio as musician with the original B. A. Rolfe Band, and who has since won distinction as an aerial photographer and Hollywood cameraman, has returned to radio as KMOX sound man. His recently finished sound table, built by himself, is the most completely equipped sound effects table in any radio station between Chicago and the west coast.

CORRECTION!

"Treasure Chest," popular children's program on KMOX each Friday at 5:15 P.M., is sponsored by the St. Louis Dairy Co. In our last issue, this program was erroneously credited to another concern.

POWER!

Cesar G. Arguenta, editor of Semanal, newspaper of Guatemala City, Central America, has written to KMOX for its weekly program lists because this station is so well and constantly received in Guatemala that his readers want regular listings of KMOX programs.
— KMOX —

2 IN 1

—he speaks in two different voices simultaneously.

For the first time on the air, or anywhere else, as far as is known, one man will speak in two entire-
(Turn to page 2)

TORCH SENSATION!

Diane Craddock—it's pronounced Dee-ahn—and "Puff" if you know her well enough—has everything it takes. Lovely face and figure, with an amazing voice that carries the torch directly to the hearts of all listeners. Diane is creating a sensation as singing star of the Union Electric Light and Power Company Show on KMOX each Thursday at 8:30 P.M.

Happy New Year

We Sincerely Hope
1934
Will Be the Greatest
12 Months
You've Ever Had

IT'S THE IDEA THAT COUNTS

STREET INTERVIEWS
SELL LAUNDRY SERVICE

Daily "Man in the Street" interviews, with France Laux, sports announcer, in a new role as interrogator, using a lapel "mike," have the people of this town talking.

Broadcast every morning except Sunday from 10:45 to 11:00 A.M., at a different spot in the city with a new question asked each day, novelty of the program locally, has all types and classes of people stopping at the previously announced broadcast spot to take part in the interviews.

Questions asked have brought some interesting answers and plenty of amusement. Among them, "Are you in favor of the return of the saloon?" rated thirteen for, and one so emphatically against that an oration had to be tactfully ended in a hurry. "What type of radio program do you like best?" found one in favor of popular music, two old-timers, two for semi-classical, one for classical, three favored dramatic programs, and one, comedy of the Burns and Allen type. Proving that good ideas are more important than new ones. "Man in the Street," patterned after Ted Husing's occasional street interviews, has in two weeks successfully sold Glick's Laundry since its sponsor, that it has continued its most confident interest.

A station newsletter from 1933 ran a short feature on one of the most talented men ever to appear on KMOX. Marvin Mueller, pictured under the "2 IN 1" headline, began working at the station while still in school at Washington University. He was a man of many voices, and he also wrote scripts for programs. Later, as a Hollywood actor, he was known as Marvin Miller. (St. Louis Media Archive.)

St. Louis Artists Bureau and Radio Training School, Inc.

CENTRAL 8240

ST. LOUIS, MO.

MART BUILDING

1932

We will be very glad to have you come in for an
audition on *Saturday May 28th*
at 8:30 o'clock, a.m.

This audition will make you elegible to appear on the
broadcast of the KMOX Public Audition Program, which
goes on the air at 9:30 o'clock, a.m. Your number will
be *10*.

It will be necessary for you to bring your own music,
or instruments; but we will provide you with an
accompanist. You are only allowed two minutes at the
most.

                    Yours very truly,

            ST. LOUIS ARTISTS BUREAU AND
              RADIO TRAINING SCHOOL.

                    Woody Klose.

WK:T   Woody Klose – Director,
                    Public Audition Committee.

KMOX announcer Woody Klose formed an artists' bureau in the Mart Building to scout for new talent. This form letter was sent to the Chassels sisters, who later formed the Harmonettes trio on KMOX. The group is seen in this book's cover photograph dressed in white evening gowns. (Sue Dorn.)

Jean Chassels also teamed with Happy Green for a weekly 15-minute-long program. (Sue Dorn.)

Another publicity photograph promoted "Happy and Bunny" for their weekly program. (Sue Dorn.)

Presentation   HASGELL AND STRAETER
Date   Wednesday   October 25, 1933
Hour   8 P. M.
Artists
Continuity   Simpson
Announcer
Approved

KMOX
The Voice of St. Louis

ANN:	Hasgell and Straeter Present:
SIG:	MUSIC MUSIC EVERYWHERE (PIANO)
ANN:	Myles Hasgell and Ted Straeter, maestros of music in St. Louis present their regular Wednesday Evening Program. Tonight Hasgell and Straeter offer------
SIG:	HARMONETTE'S THEME
ANN:	The Harmonettes.....3 young ladies with Rhythm on their minds.... First they sing of that settlement where with rings on her fingers and tears for her crown.....and that is the story of old
TRIO:	CHINATOWN MY CHINATOWN ← Carolina →
ANN:	Ted Straeter must make a piano speak.. .because it's the Talk of the Town.
TED:	TALK OF THE TOWN
ANN:	Dont feel badly Harmonettes, because while theres only one of me and theres 3 of you
TRIO:	SOME DAY SWEETHEART
ANN:	Girls, you've got to stop it...
TRIO:	LICKS
ANN:	Stop it girls, IT DONT MEAN A THING
TRIO:	IT DONT MEAN A THING
ANN:	The program's come to an end..... And those voices that so sweetly blend Are leaving you until very soon....
TRIO:	SIG
ANN:	Again on Sunday Myles Hasgell and Ted Straeter will bring you one of

Myles Hasgell and Ted Straeter owned a local talent agency that sponsored a weekly KMOX show, from which this script is taken. Every spoken word on the radio in those days had to be scripted. Ad-libbing was not allowed. (Sue Dorn.)

The formality of radio broadcasts is evident in this 1933 photograph of staff members in the Mart Building studios. (KMOX.)

After three consecutive years of winning the national championship title, Pappy Cheshire's group retired from the competition. (St. Louis Media Archive.)

150
FAVORITE RECIPES and MENUS

from

Jane Porter

and her

KMOX
MAGIC
KITCHEN

Jane Porter's Kitchen was one of the most heavily promoted programs on KMOX, with at least two cookbooks published and distributed. CBS built a fully functioning kitchen in the Mart Building and equipped it with microphones and seats for an audience. Station staff members often lined up after the program to sample the creations. (St. Louis Media Archive.)

In recognition of the outstanding services rendered by the UNITED CHARITIES in St. Louis, we are proud to do our share by presenting during the Exposition

A Galaxy of Stars

KMOX

n Feld

Al Cameron

Joe Karnes

Shumate Brothers

Margaret Daum

Howard Phillips

Emma Becker

Dell Casino

Cool

Lorraine Grimm

Pappy Cheshire and Hill Billies

Eton Boys

Robert Parsons

Harmonettes

As was often the case during the Great Depression, KMOX produced programs outside the station that were used as fundraisers for charitable causes. The shows spotlighted many of the performers heard regularly on the station. (St. Louis Media Archive.)

Self-promotion was another factor in the success of many stars and groups. Venida Jones was heard nightly on KMOX with her program of organ music. Because of its late hour, the program was popular among distant listeners, even on ships at sea, due to the signal's strength being boosted by the nighttime atmosphere. It was said she received more gifts from listeners than anyone else on the station, with the bulk of them coming from men. (St. Louis Media Archive.)

While Rita Rogers's self-promoting postcard may seem impersonal, it was practical for those artists who received hundreds of letters each week from listeners. (St. Louis Media Archive.)

RITA ROGERS—The Pevely Sunshine Girl and *"three-in-one"* artist of the air. Miss Rogers sings and whistles to her own violin accompaniment.

Dear friend:
It's fun to entertain you on the Pevely Dairy radio program every Monday, Wednesday and Friday morning at 9:45. I hope you'll tune in often.
Yours for Super-Zest
Rita Rogers

Ozark Rambler
KMOX and CBS Artist

The Ozark Rambler's promotional card was typical of those artists who participated in several different programs. Some were broadcast only on KMOX, and other shows were heard only on the CBS Network. (St. Louis Media Archive.)

Rather than sending out promotional postcards, the popular Ozark Mountaineers produced a number of high-quality 8-by-10-inch photographs, which were sent to fans. (St. Louis Media Archive.)

An unidentified hillbilly group poses with a KMOX staff announcer in the Mart Building studios. The station had recently acquired a new, less obtrusive style of microphone. (St. Louis Media Archive.)

The Novelty Boys had several different promotional cards over the three years they were employed at KMOX. In the early 1940s, after working at several radio stations in other cities, the pair returned to KMOX with a larger group and stayed only a few months until Jimmie went into the military service in 1943. (St. Louis Media Archive.)

The *Singercrafters* weekly program, sponsored by the Singer Sewing Machine Company, was promoted with postcards like this one. (St. Louis Media Archive.)

Uncle Feezel's sponsor, the International Heating Oil Company, printed up special ink blotters. (St. Louis Media Archive.)

They were originally Henry, Zeb, and Otto. Then a personnel change begat Buddy, Zeb, and Otto, and their sponsor was Purina. Otto also was leader of Herr Otto's Little German Band on KMOX. (St. Louis Media Archive.)

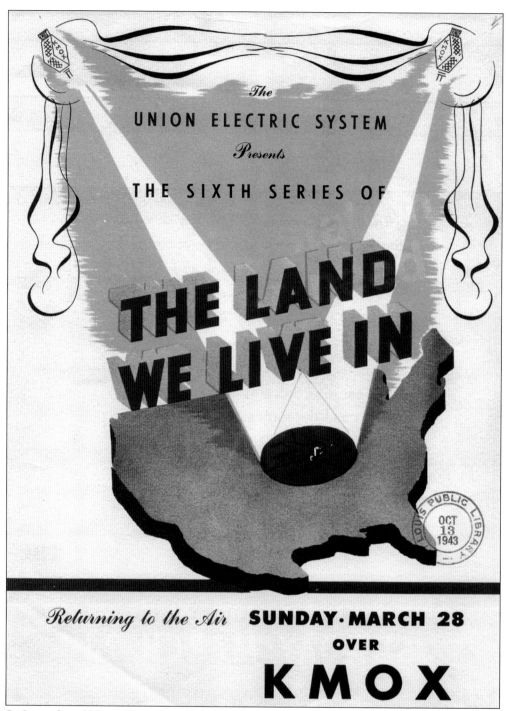

St. Louis–based Union Electric sponsored the long-running weekly dramatic program *The Land We Live In*, which presented recreations of local history. Weekly live productions of the show were a massive undertaking, from composition and orchestration of original music scores to hiring local actors, not to mention the research and writing. Production quality was on a par with anything broadcast from New York. (St. Louis Media Archive.)

"The Phillips 66 Saturday Night Club"
I was MC with Al Roth's orchestra.
The CBS Playhouse Auditorium Studio.

The lavish *Phillips 66 Saturday Night Club* productions in the Mart Building auditorium were also a challenge, with presentations by many local musicians. (St. Louis Media Archive.)

The *Church of the Air* program was broadcast weekly on CBS beginning in 1931. It featured performances of musical groups from different cities around the United States. This group is pictured singing on a national hookup from the Mart Building studios. (Library of American Broadcasting, University of Maryland.)

OL' CHUCK AND JOE KARNES

The musical comedy team of Ol' Chuck and Joe Karnes distributed this publicity photograph. (St. Louis Media Archive.)

In 1935, The Ozark Mountaineers sent out this photograph to their fans. (St. Louis Media Archive.)

France Laux, shown here during spring training, became the major sports voice of KMOX and of CBS. In addition to broadcasting the games of the St. Louis Cardinals and Browns, he was called upon for national broadcasts of the World Series and all-star games and hosted regular sports programs on KMOX. (St. Louis Media Archive.)

Ken Wright came to KMOX in 1932 as the station's daytime organist, so one of his main jobs was filling dead air until announcers or performers were ready. His organ music provided background music and created moods and aural transitions for the station's programs. He was also Sad Sam the Accordian Man, performing with Sunny Joe Wolverton's group. (St. Louis Media Archive.)

Presentation HOME FOLKS HOUR
Date   11/27/34
Hour   5;30 to 7;15
Artists WT;OZ:SK:HM;JIM:B&H;MA
Continuity CS
Announcer   CS
Approved

KMOX
The Voice of St. Louis

5;30		FARMYARD RECORD AND SIGN ON
	OZARKS:	OLD GREY BONNET
	OZARKS:	DOWN YONDER
	M.ANN:	WOULD YOU CARE
	B&H:	SMILE DARN YOU SMILE
	SKEETS:	MISS.VALLEY BLUES
	H.MEN:	SWANEE RIVER MOON
5;45	WEATHER REPORT & QUESTIONS	
	OZARKS:	BEAUTIFUL OHIO
	JIM:	BURGLAR MAN SONG
	SKEETS:	FALLING LEAVES
6;00	PERUNA	
6;15	PROF.LEE.A.SOMERS U.OF I.	
6;23	B&H:	CUT DOWN OLD PINE TREE
6;25	WEATHER--MARKETS	
6;30	DIX.HB:	SONG
	M.ANN:	LITTLE DARLING PAL OF MINE
	H?MEN:	YOU CAN'T FOOL AN OLD HOSSFLY
6;45	GERMANIA(Wright-Organ)	
7;00	KOLOR BAK	

***   ***

This is the program rundown for a 1934 hillbilly show. Music groups included the Ozark Mountaineers, Melody Ann, Skeets Yaney, the Dixie Hillbillies, and Ken Wright. Once this document was completed, the KMOX continuity department would write the script for the show. (St. Louis Media Archive.)

This promotional photograph for the *Farm Folks Hour* was distributed by the station and by sponsor Bristol Myers. Farm director Ted Mangner is shown in the middle of the group. (St. Louis Media Archive.)

Pappy Cheshire's talented group, seen in this image, was a sizable one. For a while, their live music could be heard at 6:00 in the morning and at 10:30 in the evening, so one can speculate that he divided the chores so the workload was reasonable. The group also made many personal appearances at numerous country fairs in Missouri and Illinois. (St. Louis Media Archive.)

Four

LEAVING THE GREAT DEPRESSION BEHIND

Harry Flannery was the first well-known broadcast journalist on KMOX. He worked at the station from 1935 to 1939 and became something of a celebrity for his efforts. Flannery was tapped by CBS to succeed William Shirer when the latter left Berlin in 1940 to return to network news headquarters. Following his work as a war correspondent, Flannery went to KNX in Los Angeles. (St. Louis Media Archive.)

"WADE RAY and his GANG"

Lester (Lullaby) Maeberry   Eddie (Cat-Fish) Gentry   Stuffy (Egg Shell) Austin   Robert (Brother Bob) Hastings

Wade Ray

YOUR KMOX COUNTRY JOURNAL ENTERTAINERS

To promote the KMOX *Country Journal* in 1945, KMOX recycled an earlier photograph of Wade Ray's group (shown on page 36) and provided some additional writing. (St. Louis Media Archive.)

Sally Foster was a very popular hillbilly singer on KMOX, who later became Little Blue-eyed Sally on the *National Barn Dance* program on WLS in Chicago. (St. Louis Media Archive.)

THE ST. LOUIS STATION OF THE COLUMBIA BROADCASTING SYSTEM

KMOX

50,000 WATTS, 1120 KILOCYCLES · 401 SOUTH TWELFTH STREET, ST. LOUIS 2, MISSOURI

ADDENDA TO RATE CARD NO. 18 · EFFECTIVE AUGUST 20, 1944

1. Participating Announcement Programs

a. KMOX COUNTRY JOURNAL: Monday thru Saturday, 5:30-7:00 a.m.
Rates for one hour, one half-hour or one quarter-hour as shown under Section I, Class "E."

PARTICIPATIONS:	*1 TIME	*13 TIMES	*26 OR MORE TIMES
100 words live or 40 second transcriptions...........	$28.00	$22.00	$16.00
One minute live or transcribed......................	42.00	33.00	24.00
*Times within 1 year.			

Cannot be combined with other service for further discounts.

LIVESTOCK AND MARKET REPORTS, FARM SERVICE FEATURES OR NEWS: Approximately five minutes in the Country Journal, prepared and presented by the KMOX Farm Director. Three times weekly: $150.00. Six times weekly: $250.00.
Cannot be combined with other service for further discounts.

b. KMOX MAGIC KITCHEN: Fifteen minute participating program, written and presented by Jane Porter, KMOX Home Economist. Participation consists of one minute live announcement (daily) plus opening, middle and closing announcements on one complete sponsorship day per week. Participation $200.00 per week.
Cannot be combined with other service for further discounts.

c. All above rates for participations are subject to agency commission. No further discounts.

2. News Services

a. Complete press and radio wire services of Press Association (AP) and UP available. Rates on application.

3. Length of Commercial Copy

LENGTH OF PROGRAM	BEFORE 6 p. m.	NEWS BEFORE 6 p. m.	AFTER 6 p. m.	NEWS AFTER 6 p. m.
5 minutes................. 1:25		1:08	1:10	:56
10 minutes................. 2:20		1:52	1:50	1:28
15 minutes................. 3:15		2:36	2:30	2:00
30 minutes................. 4:30		3:36	3:00	2:24
60 minutes................. 9:00			6:00	

Special regulations on News Programs regarding commercial copy:

1. Maximum opening commercial: 25 seconds for 5-minute news program, 40 seconds for 10-minute program or longer. 2. No middle commercial permitted on 5-minute news program.

4. Commercial Rates for Musicians

a. Rates on application.

5. Special Rates for Announcement Packages

a. No Announcement Packages available on KMOX.

6. Announcer Costs

a. Rates on application.

7. Instantaneous Reference Recordings*

a. PRICE: $7.50 each, net, per 15 minute unit or less.
*Current ruling of the American Federation of Musicians makes it impossible to record musical programs.

Although the world was at war in 1944, commercial radio stations were thriving. They became the primary source for war news for many people, thanks to Edward R. Murrow and his trusted band of CBS correspondents. The rate card for KMOX shows how much the station charged for advertising in that era. (St. Louis Media Archive.)

In a major fundraising effort during the war, KMOX teamed up with the *Globe-Democrat*. (Library of American Broadcasting, University of Maryland.)

Wet streets from an earlier rain did not stop these citizens from participating in the Mile of Dimes promotion in 1944. (St. Louis Media Archive.)

Curt Ray personally judges all song requests to assure a smooth 30 minutes of music over KMOX at 8:00 AM each weekday morning

RHYME DOES PAY

Popular emcee Curt Ray keeps the rhymes and records rolling on "Rhyme Does Pay"

KMOX Disc Show Broadcasts Your Own Favorites, Offers Cash Awards for Song Requests in Rhyme

One of the most popular record shows winging through the St. Louis ozone these days is "Rhyme Does Pay"—heard over KMOX each morning at 8:00 AM. Emceed by Curt Ray, who knows his music from A to Z, "Rhyme Does Pay" features cash awards for record requests written in rhyme, and adds up to a highly listenable half-hour of good fun and good music.

It's the sort of show "Prom" readers will go for—so don't miss it. Better yet, join the fun yourself and send Curt Ray your own request. If yours is one of the five daily winners, Curt will play your favorite recording, broadcast your jingle and send you a buck in the bargain.

Just write your request in the form of a rhyme, ending with the title of a popular song—and if you wish, add the name of your school, club or fraternity when you sign your own name and address.

Don't forget to listen in each weekday morning at 8:00 AM—you'll find the listening's fine.

KMOX THE VOICE OF ST. LOUIS **1120 ON YOUR DIAL**

By 1947, KMOX was even courting a teenage audience, as seen in this advertisement from *Prom Magazine*. Disc jockey Curt Ray made numerous personal appearances at local schools and developed a following among the teen music audience. (St. Louis Media Archive.)

Vox Pop was an enormously popular comedy/variety program heard each week on CBS. Hosts Parks Johnson and Warren Hull traveled to different cities for the show, which spotlighted audience participation and quiz questions for prizes. This 1944 photograph is from one of three *Vox Pop* programs broadcast from St. Louis. (Library of American Broadcasting, University of Maryland.)

In 1946, Frank Zwygart came to town. At his last radio job in Cincinnati, he went by the name Rex Davis, which he carried over to his new job at KMOX. In his 35 years here, Davis became the voice of radio news in St. Louis, winning many national awards for his work. (St. Louis Media Archive.)

After the war, construction projects that had been stalled sprang up everywhere. CBS invested in a large plot of land northeast of St. Louis and began work on a new transmitter building. (KMOX.)

Due to a postwar shortage of materials, CBS opted to recycle an old radio tower for KMOX, transporting it from co-owned WBBM in Chicago. (KMOX.)

A radio station newsletter from 1949 offered readers a visual tour of the new transmitter building and tower site located in a field near Stallings, Illinois. (St. Louis Media Archive.)

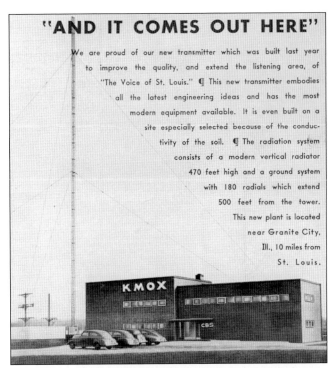

"AND IT COMES OUT HERE"

We are proud of our new transmitter which was built last year to improve the quality, and extend the listening area, of "The Voice of St. Louis." ❡ This new transmitter embodies all the latest engineering ideas and has the most modern equipment available. It is even built on a site especially selected because of the conductivity of the soil. ❡ The radiation system consists of a modern vertical radiator 470 feet high and a ground system with 180 radials which extend 500 feet from the tower. This new plant is located near Granite City, Ill., 10 miles from St. Louis.

The master control desk sat in front of the huge radio transmitter in the two-story building. Broadcast engineers remained on duty at the console at all times the station was on the air. (St. Louis Media Archive.)

ESSENTIAL!

in the lives of the citizens
of a great metropolitan area

"The Voice of St. Louis"

By the end of the 1940s, the radio industry was facing a new reality. Its previous big-name stars were making the transition to television, leaving the radio networks struggling for programming. Radio stations began to originate a larger percentage of their broadcast schedules. Within the next decade, KMOX, under new general manager Robert Hyland, would remake itself into a radio station that would provide programs for every taste. (St. Louis Media Archive.)

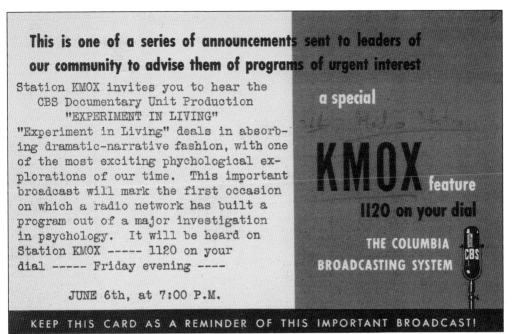

This is one of a series of announcements sent to leaders of our community to advise them of programs of urgent interest

Station KMOX invites you to hear the CBS Documentary Unit Production "EXPERIMENT IN LIVING"

"Experiment in Living" deals in absorbing dramatic-narrative fashion, with one of the most exciting phychological explorations of our time. This important broadcast will mark the first occasion on which a radio network has built a program out of a major investigation in psychology. It will be heard on Station KMOX ----- 1120 on your dial ----- Friday evening ----

JUNE 6th, at 7:00 P.M.

a special

KMOX feature

1120 on your dial

THE COLUMBIA BROADCASTING SYSTEM

KEEP THIS CARD AS A REMINDER OF THIS IMPORTANT BROADCAST!

On a few occasions, KMOX would use direct mail to target a specific audience, informing them of a particular program on the coming schedule. (St. Louis Media Archive.)

"TED" "REX" "HOWARD"

KMOX - CBS

As the 1940s drew to a close, the station's morning broadcast team consisted of Ted Mangner, Rex Davis, and Howard Dorsey. (St. Louis Media Archive.)

Harry Caray joined KMOX in 1954 as the play-by-play announcer for the St. Louis Cardinals. (St. Louis Media Archive.)

The relationship between the Cardinals and KMOX was to span five continuous decades. (St. Louis Media Archive.)

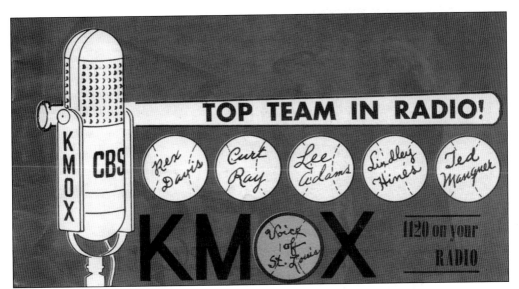

Even though St. Louis Browns games were broadcast on another radio station, advertisements like this one for KMOX could be found in the programs sold at Browns games in the early 1950s. (St. Louis Media Archive.)

In 1950, a young staff announcer/ musician named Ollie Raymand joined KMOX. (St. Louis Media Archive.)

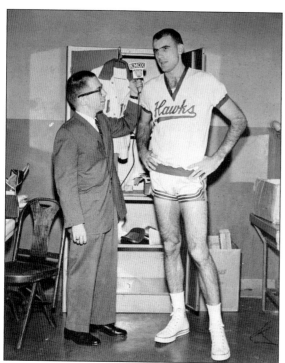

Jim Butler was hired as an announcer in 1951. He is shown here interviewing Bob Petit of the St. Louis Hawks. (St. Louis Media Archive.)

This scene from the station's flood coverage in the 1950s is indicative of the growing importance of local news to the station and its listeners. (St. Louis Media Archive.)

The pursuit of teenage music listeners continued on KMOX in 1954 with the weekend program *Teen O'Clock Time*. The show featured weekly school salutes and remote broadcasts from local auditoriums. (St. Louis Media Archive.)

THIS...

KMOX
AND
VANDERVOORT'S
cordially invite you to attend
YOUR *High School's*
"Teen O'Clock Time"
and
"Dance"
Saturday afternoon
CHASE CLUB OF THE HOTEL CHASE
one-thirty until five
Informal
THIS INVITATION MUST BE PRESENTED AT THE DOOR

...Is an invitation to the big, new "Teen o'Clock Time"... A wonderful Saturday afternoon party of fun, dancing and entertainment featuring Curt Ray, master-of-ceremonies, leading a parade of outstanding high school talent, a dancing party, fashion show, new record releases, prizes, refreshments, the CBS-Network broadcast of "Saturday at the Chase"... PLUS the opportunity to see and meet "in-person" top stars of radio, stage and screen. Stan Daugherty and the 21-piece KMOX orchestra; Tommye Birch, fashion commentator; and Willard Scott, announcer, will also be featured in this gala party at the Chase Club.

Watch for your invitation when "Teen o'Clock Time" salutes your school
Listen to "Teen o'Clock Time," Saturdays at 4:00 to 5:00 p.m. on KMOX
And be sure to tell your friends and parents about it!

CBS Radio   **KMOX**   The Voice of St. Louis
                 50,000 watts, dial 1120

Disc jockey Curt Ray maintained a large following from the young audience in the 1950s. (St. Louis Media Archive.)

Bob Burnes, sports columnist for the *Globe-Democrat*, joined KMOX in 1947 and is believed to have later hosted the station's first call-in sports program. (St. Louis Media Archive.)

When his career as a Major League Baseball player ended, home-towner Joe Garagiola joined the KMOX sports department. (St. Louis Media Archive.)

ST. LOUIS MART BUILDING, ST. LOUIS, MO.—99

By the mid-1950s, KMOX management and ownership faced some unforeseen problems. The station's landlord at the Mart Building told CBS the lease would not be renewed because the federal government needed the floor space. CBS was in the process of establishing a television station in St. Louis and contemplated putting the two operations into a new combined facility, but the radio station was forced to move before anything could be built. In 1957, KMOX relocated to the vacant Anthony and Kuhn Brewery complex in the Soulard neighborhood south of downtown. No photographs have been found of any of the station's large facilities there. CBS finally decided to put the TV station in a stand-alone building and construct new studios for KMOX. The radio station remained in the brewery complex for three years. (St. Louis Media Archive.)

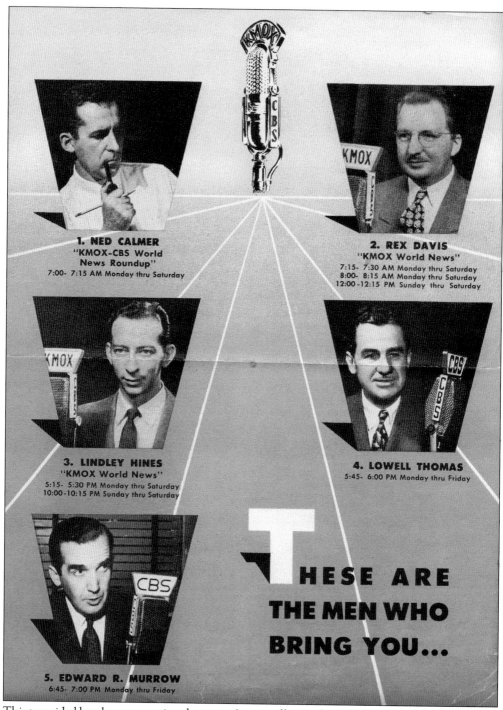

1. NED CALMER
"KMOX-CBS World
News Roundup"
7:00- 7:15 AM Monday thru Saturday

2. REX DAVIS
"KMOX World News"
7:15- 7:30 AM Monday thru Saturday
8:00- 8:15 AM Monday thru Saturday
12:00 -12:15 PM Sunday thru Saturday

3. LINDLEY HINES
"KMOX World News"
5:15- 5:30 PM Monday thru Saturday
10:00-10:15 PM Sunday thru Saturday

4. LOWELL THOMAS
5:45- 6:00 PM Monday thru Friday

5. EDWARD R. MURROW
6:45- 7:00 PM Monday thru Friday

THESE ARE
THE MEN WHO
BRING YOU...

This two-sided brochure promoting the station's news effort in the 1950s emphasized the combined

KMOX CBS NEWS

Up-to-the-minute, unbiased, on-the-spot, factual news!

12:00 Noon (Sunday thru Saturday)
Sun., Tues., & Thurs. Sponsored by PETER PAUL MOUNDS & ALMOND JOY
Mon., Wed., & Fri. Sponsored by NUTRENA MILLS
Sat. Sponsored by JACK KENNEDY CHEVROLET CO.

1. NED CALMER
"KMOX-CBS WORLD NEWS ROUNDUP"
7:00 AM (Monday thru Saturday)
Led by Ned Calmer in New York and featuring on-the-spot reports from CBS correspondents all over the world.
Sponsored by STANDARD OIL AGENTS AND DEALERS

2. REX DAVIS
"KMOX WORLD NEWS"
7:15 AM (Monday thru Saturday)
Mon., Wed., & Fri. Sponsored by DOLCIN
Tues., Thurs., Sat. Sponsored by the makers of MENNEN PRODUCTS FOR MEN

8:00 AM (Monday thru Saturday)
Mon., Wed., & Fri. Sponsored by SHELL OIL COMPANY
Tues., Thurs., & Sat. Sponsored by WESTINGHOUSE

3. LINDLEY HINES
"KMOX WORLD NEWS"
5:15 PM (Monday thru Saturday)
Mon., Wed., & Fri. Sponsored by FOLGER'S COFFEE
Tues., Thurs., & Sat. Sponsored by STUDEBAKER

10:00 PM (Sunday thru Saturday)
Sponsored by STANDARD OIL AGENTS AND DEALERS

4. LOWELL THOMAS
5:45-6:00 PM (Monday thru Friday)
Sponsored by the makers of IVORY SOAP

5. EDWARD R. MURROW
6:45-7:00 PM (Monday thru Friday)
Radio's Most Honored Reporter brings you fifteen minutes of up-to-the-minute news and its significance.

TODAY ... MORE PEOPLE DEPEND ON RADIO FOR NEWS ... AND MORE ST. LOUISANS DEPEND UPON ...

KMOX "THE VOICE OF ST. LOUIS"

efforts of KMOX and CBS. (St. Louis Media Archive.)

Harry Caray's popularity continued to soar, especially after the St. Louis Browns moved to Baltimore in 1954. (St. Louis Media Archive.)

KMOX was also the home of the NBA's St. Louis Hawks game broadcasts by Buddy Blattner and Jim Butler. (St. Louis Media Archive.)

Harry Fender, a former star in the *Ziegfeld Follies*, joined the KMOX staff as a program host in 1954. (St. Louis Media Archive.)

Local and national celebrities joined KMOX announcers to raise funds to fight cancer in 1957. (St. Louis Media Archive.)

KMOX chief engineer Larry Burrows posed in front of some of the station's electronic equipment in 1959. (St. Louis Mercantile Library Association.)

This emergency backup studio was at the transmitter site. It also contained emergency water and food supplies for the staff. (KMOX.)

By 1958, land had been found for construction of the new KMOX radio studios on the northeast corner of Hampton and Wise Avenues. The changing radio programming scene meant there was no more demand for live program productions, so the building was much smaller than those the station had previously occupied. In 1961, KMOX-FM signed on, but separate studios were not needed since most of the programming was a duplicated broadcast of what was on the AM station. The stations' general manager, Robert Hyland, focused on making the offices a showcase for what radio was to become. (KMOX.)

KMOX

CBS Radio—A Division of Columbia Broadcasting System, Inc.

1144 HAMPTON AVENUE, ST. LOUIS, MISSOURI 63139 STerling 1-2345

Nov . 23, 1965

KMOX moved into its new facility on August 31, 1959. (St. Louis Media Archive.)

CBS executives traveled to St. Louis for the dedication of the building, which was the first the company had constructed exclusively for radio in over 20 years. (St. Louis Mercantile Library Association.)

Decor in the Hampton offices reflected the Spartan tastes of the 1950s. (St. Louis Media Archive.)

News director Rex Davis is shown in the newsroom with members of his staff. The staffer on the right is checking the news service teletype, which was housed in a special cabinet to muffle its noise. (St. Louis Mercantile Library Association.)

Studios were configured for call-in programs, and the producer in the foreground screened the calls. Engineers are shown behind the plate glass window. (St. Louis Media Archive.)

Bruce Hayward is seen hosting a record program as his engineer handles the technical responsibilities. Production studios are visible in the background. (St. Louis Media Archive.)

The station's record library on Hampton was overseen by music director Larry Torno (right). (St. Louis Media Archive.)

It became a standing joke among all KMOX staffers during the entire tenure of Robert Hyland as KMOX general manager that his desk was always clean. (St. Louis Media Archive.)

Former Cardinals catcher Joe Garagiola was in the booth with play-by-play man Harry Caray in 1960. (St. Louis Media Archive.)

All three members of the Cardinals announcing staff—Jack Buck, Harry Caray, and Joe Garagiola—were later honored with the Baseball Hall of Fame's Ford C. Frick Award. (St. Louis Media Archive.)

Station staffers, including Robert Hyland, were regular participants in the annual *Globe-Democrat* Old Newsboys' Day. (Molly Hyland.)

In honor of farm director Ted Mangner's 20th anniversary with the station, Robert Hyland helped Mangner cut the cake. (St. Louis Media Archive.)

John McCormick, whose demeanor and on-air presentation were reminiscent of radio's golden days, joined KMOX in 1959. (St. Louis Media Archive.)

Bruce Hayward's long St. Louis broadcast career spanned radio and television positions. He joined KMOX in 1958. (St. Louis Media Archive.)

J. Roy McCarthy, a former schoolteacher, was hired in 1960 to become one of the first regular hosts of the new KMOX talk format known as "At Your Service." (St. Louis Media Archive.)

When this publicity photograph was taken, this man was known as Grant Williams. Later, on other stations and during a second stint at KMOX, the public knew him as Grant Horton. (St. Louis Media Archive.)

The "At Your Service" programming brought experts and newsmakers to the KMOX airwaves and gave listeners a chance to phone in their questions and comments. (St. Louis Media Archive.)

KMOX personality Bob Anthony is shown at the station's booth during a promotion. Participants were given a small acetate record of their interview. (KMOX.)

Jack Buck and Robert Hyland pose in the "At Your Service" studio with former first lady Eleanor Roosevelt. (St. Louis Media Archive.)

As soon as the "At Your Service" format was in place, management held daily meetings to discuss possible guests. Shown from left to right are Jim Butler, Bob Hardy, Robert Hyland, and Rex Davis. (Molly Hyland.)

By the mid-1960s, downtown St. Louis was in the midst of a construction boom, spurred by the Gateway Arch on the riverfront. KMOX news provided the public with regular reports of its progress, giving journalists like Bob Hardy some very challenging assignments. (St. Louis Media Archive.)

Baseball announcer Jack Buck wore many hats at the station, also serving as a host for "At Your Service." (St. Louis Media Archive.)

Harry Fender held down evening programming from the Chase Hotel, interviewing celebrities. He is shown here on the left with the Three Stooges. (St. Louis Media Archive.)

Now ON KMOX RADIO

the Jack Buck Show now from the new Musial and Biggie's

nightly 10:15 to midnight

DIAL 1120

THE VOICE OF ST. LOUIS

Buck's nights were busy, too. When not broadcasting from the booth at Busch Stadium or traveling with the Cardinals, he hosted a nightly program from one of the city's most popular restaurants. (St. Louis Media Archive.)

Under the oversight of news director Rex Davis, KMOX was becoming more deeply ingrained in the community, producing in-depth reports that won many national awards. Here, reporter Bill Fields works on a series about life in the city's slums. (St. Louis Media Archive.)

Old Newsboys' Day KMOX staffers on Hampton Avenue included Jack Buck, Taffy Wilber, Jim Butler, and Skip Caray. (St. Louis Media Archive.)

This promotional display at a local function in 1965 gave the public a chance to listen to radio history. (St. Louis Media Archive.)

It became a tradition at KMOX for the boss to appear as an "At Your Service" guest each year on the anniversary of the program's inaugural broadcast to take questions and comments from listeners. (St. Louis Media Archive.)

After about 10 years in the Hampton studios, KMOX was on the move again. This time, the station headed back downtown, where all the construction activity had included a building with the best view in the city. (St. Louis Media Archive.)

Five

SHIFTING GEARS
FOR THE FUTURE

The fashionable-sounding address was 1 Memorial Drive, although the entrance was on Market Street. From the studios on the building's third floor, broadcasters and guests could gaze out over the grounds of the Gateway Arch and across the Mississippi River through the outer walls of floor-to-ceiling glass. The KMOX studio complex in this building also included facilities for KMOX-FM on the seventh floor and KMOX-TV on the first floor. For the first time, all local CBS properties were housed in the same building. (St. Louis Media Archive.)

The new master control room had studios on two sides and a backup control facility in the next room. (KMOX.)

The backup control facility is shown in this photograph of the main studio at Memorial Drive. In addition, there was a news booth to the side and two more studios nearby. (St. Louis Media Archive.)

KMOX general manager and CBS vice president Robert Hyland had presided over the steady development of the station, and its move to the prestigious downtown location was indicative of just how far the station had come under his leadership. (Molly Hyland.)

TIME	MONDAY - FRIDAY	SATURDAY	SUNDAY
6 AM–9 AM	**TOTAL INFORMATION** Mort Crowley - Bob Hardy - Rex Davis - Jack Buck - Bob Starr News, Weather, Sports, CBS Features TRAFFIC/SAFETY REPORTS with Don Miller	TOTAL INFORMATION News, Weather Sports TRADING STATION Jack Carney	MUSIC NEWS RELIGION
9 AM–1 PM	**JACK CARNEY SHOW** KMOX Local/CBS News and Features	Jack Carney Saturday Show KMOX/CBS News & Features SPORTS OPEN LINE	KMOX/CBS NEWS ON A SUNDAY MORNING
1 PM–5 PM	**AT YOUR SERVICE** Guest-Experts — Comments and Questions from Listeners KMOX Local/CBS News and Features	CARDINAL BASEBALL MISSOURI U. "TIGER" FOOTBALL CARDINAL FOOTBALL SPIRITS BASKETBALL	
5 PM–8 PM	**CBS News/KMOX News and Weather** Financial News - Sports Digest - CBS Features AT YOUR SERVICE - SPORTS OPEN LINE TRAFFIC/SAFETY REPORTS with Don Miller	KMOX/CBS NEWS SPORTS FEATURES MUSIC ON A SATURDAY EVENING	MUSIC ON A SUNDAY EVENING NEWS CBS FEATURES
8 PM–12 M	**CARDINAL BASEBALL/BLUES HOCKEY SPIRITS BASKETBALL** AT YOUR SERVICE/KMOX and CBS NETWORK NEWS **CBS RADIO MYSTERY THEATER**	CARDINAL BASEBALL BLUES HOCKEY POP CONCERT	
12 M–6 AM	**"THE MAN WHO WALKS AND TALKS AT MIDNIGHT"** John McCormick	MAN WHO WALKS AND TALKS AT MIDNIGHT KMOX/CBS NEWS	MAN WHO WALKS AND TALKS AT MIDNIGHT KMOX/CBS NEWS

KMOX RADIO

1120
ON YOUR DIAL
C B S

A station program schedule shows that the talk format had become dominant, with only the late-night hours dedicated to music. (St. Louis Media Archive.)

WHAT MAKES KMOX RADIO TOTAL ENTERTAINMENT?

In its external promotion, the station often wisely focused on its personalities. Each person was intelligent, community oriented, and friendly, causing many listeners to view them as part of the family. That familial relationship became an integral part of the station's identity. Everyone who worked there was perceived as part of the successful radio team. (St. Louis Media Archive.)

Jim White joined the KMOX team in 1969. He is best remembered as the host of late-night call-in shows. (KMOX.)

NIGHTTIME: AT YOUR SERVICE on KMOX RADIO

Those late-night shows were patterned after the call-in programs heard during the day—all part of the "At Your Service" brand of talk radio. (St. Louis Media Archive.)

Rex Davis, who had served as KMOX news director, was relieved of those duties so he could take a high-profile on-air role. He became part of the two-man *Total Information* AM morning show. (St. Louis Media Archive.)

Bob Hardy served as Rex Davis's coanchor on *Total Information* AM. Together, they dominated St. Louis morning radio, often registering listenership that totaled one-third of the entire morning drive-time audience. (St. Louis Media Archive.)

John McCormick, who provided overnight music for the huge national audience of KMOX, was known as "The Man Who Walks and Talks at Midnight." (St. Louis Media Archive.)

During the 1973 newspaper strike in St. Louis, Stan "The Man" Musial became a fixture on KMOX as he read the daily comic strips to listeners. (St. Louis Media Archive.)

Jack Carney, who had been a disc jockey in St. Louis in the late 1950s, came to KMOX in 1971. His morning program that followed *Total Information AM* continued the station's market dominance among listeners. (St. Louis Media Archive.)

Bill King and Norma Sacks (second and third from left), who won a contest on Jack Carney's (shown wearing hat) program, were married May 21, 1983, following Carney's parade through Forest Park. (Bill and Norma King.)

Miriam Blue, a cleaning lady at KMOX in the 1970s and 1980s, became one of the station's most beloved personalities after Jack Carney invited her to sit down and talk during his program. One of her regular features on the show was an advice segment in which she humorously answered questions from listeners, ending the segment with her trademark, "All is well!" (St. Louis Media Archive.)

A program producer and technical engineer prepare for an hour of "At Your Service" programming. The stacked items are tape cartridges containing commercials for broadcast. (St. Louis Media Archive.)

RICHARD HAYMAN AT THE POPS
Date Of Broadcast: SUNDAY, SEPT. 11,1977 KMOX (Section #1)

NAME OF SELECTION	NAME OF ALBUM & ARTIST	LENGTH OF SELECTION
1. STRUNG OUT (Theme)	Strung Out (Gordon Staples) Motown MS 722	1:00
2. FESTIVE OVERTURE (Shostakowitch)	Fiedlers Favorite Overtures (Boston Pops) Polydor 24-5006	5:32
Voice Over INTRO To Comm. (CUTAWAY)		(6:32)
3. DIE FLEDERMAUS OVERTURE (J. Strauss)	Viennese Night at the Proms Sir John Barbirolli Mercury MG 50124	7:20
4. VIENNA, CITY OF MY DREAMS (Sieczynski)	The Worlds Great Waltzes (Fiedler/ BPO) RCA CSC 0604	3:20
2 Voice Over (CUTAWAY)		(10:40)
5. CHAMPAGNE POLKA, Opus 211 (Strauss)	Tales from Vienna (Fiedler/BPO) RCA LSC 2928	2:45
6. BACCHANALE from SAMSON & DELILAH (Saint Saens)	Opera Ballets (Pro Musica Symphony; Vienna) VOX PL 9550	7:15
Voice (CUTAWAY)		(10:00)
7. POMP & CIRCUMSTANCE MARCH #1 (Elgar)	Worlds Greatest Marches (Fiedler/ BPO) RCA LSC 2757	5:35
8. ABU HASSAN OVERTURE (Carl Maria Von Weber)	Great Overtures (Scherchen) Westminster WMS 1021	3:02
		(8:37)
CLOSE		
If more time needed, use Theme STRUNG OUT (#1) to fill		
	Total	35:49

Robert Hyland continued his tradition in the Memorial Drive studios of appearing as a guest on "At Your Service." (Molly Hyland.)

Music lists were prepared for every program on KMOX, as this example for guest announcer Richard Hayman of the St. Louis Symphony shows. Pencil markings were made by the engineer. The ballpoint pen markings in the right margins represent the total music time for each segment. (St. Louis Media Archive.)

Don Miller, a former St. Louis police officer, became the voice of airborne traffic reports on KMOX in 1971 and held the job for over two decades. (St. Louis Media Archive.)

The play-by-play team of Jack Buck and Mike Shannon is shown here in their broadcast position at Busch Stadium in 1989. (St. Louis Media Archive.)

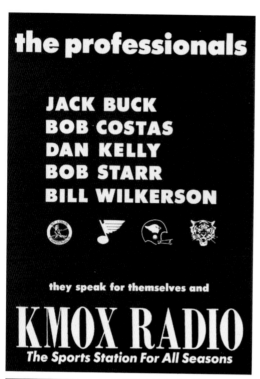

the professionals

JACK BUCK
BOB COSTAS
DAN KELLY
BOB STARR
BILL WILKERSON

they speak for themselves and

KMOX RADIO
The Sports Station For All Seasons

In addition to being known for its strong news department, KMOX assembled what many considered to be the best team of sports announcers in the country. (St. Louis Media Archive.)

In the mid-1980s, Bob Costas had left his job at KMOX for a job with NBC, but many still considered him a part of the KMOX family. From left to right are Dan Dierdorf, Bob Costas, Harry Caray, and Bill Wilkerson at Busch Stadium for a radio feature he called the *Friday Frank Forecast*. (St. Louis Media Archive.)

After Rex Davis retired, the *Total Information* AM morning team was Bill Wilkerson, Wendy Wiese, and Bob Hardy. (St. Louis Media Archive.)

Anne Keefe joined KMOX in 1977 and stayed until her retirement 16 years later. A favorite of all her coworkers, she was known as a straight shooter both on and off the air. (KMOX.)

Carol Daniel was hired as a news anchor/reporter in 1995. (St. Louis Media Archive.)

Robert Hyland is shown accepting a Peabody Award, one of several the station has received. It is considered the most prestigious award in the broadcast business. (Molly Hyland.)

Late in his KMOX career, Rex Davis made occasional appearances on Jack Carney's program, often in his persona as poet Percy Dovetonsils. (KMOX.)

Jim White is shown being interviewed by newswoman Carol Daniel as Jim's longtime producer Elaine Stern looks on. (KMOX.)

In addition to providing broadcast segments of the event, KMOX always had a visual presence in the annual Great Forest Park Balloon Race. (KMOX.)

With the reputation and talent KMOX had in sports coverage, this slogan was not an exaggeration. (St. Louis Media Archive.)

For years, this was the first thing drivers saw once they reached the west side of the Poplar Street Bridge over the Mississippi River coming into St. Louis. The brevity and simplicity of the message were indicative of just how well known KMOX was in the region. The sign didn't even bother advertising the station's dial position. (St. Louis Media Archive.)

This advertisement provides another example of a statement of fact rather than braggadocio. KMOX, the Voice of St. Louis, was one of the few stations anywhere that could legitimately claim it had everything a radio listener might want. (St. Louis Media Archive.)

Most print advertisements run by the station since the 1960s have been simple in message, conveying a basic idea: that KMOX was the only station listeners would ever need. (St. Louis Media Archive.)

ABOUT THE
ST. LOUIS MEDIA
HISTORY FOUNDATION

The St. Louis Media History Foundation was formed to accumulate and preserve media history and artifacts. Working in conjunction with area institutions such as the St. Louis Public Library Media Archive, the foundation continues to promote the storied past of media in the St. Louis area.

St. Louis Media History Foundation
2011 Virginia Avenue
Saint Louis, Missouri 63104-1524
314-537-1500
www.stlradio.com

DISCOVER THOUSANDS OF LOCAL HISTORY BOOKS FEATURING MILLIONS OF VINTAGE IMAGES

Arcadia Publishing, the leading local history publisher in the United States, is committed to making history accessible and meaningful through publishing books that celebrate and preserve the heritage of America's people and places.

Find more books like this at
www.arcadiapublishing.com

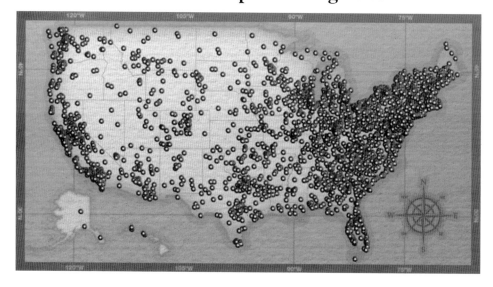

Search for your hometown history, your old stomping grounds, and even your favorite sports team.

Consistent with our mission to preserve history on a local level, this book was printed in South Carolina on American-made paper and manufactured entirely in the United States. Products carrying the accredited Forest Stewardship Council (FSC) label are printed on 100 percent FSC-certified paper.

MADE IN THE  USA